Larry Burkett's

ALL ABOUT MONEY

Discovering the History, Purpose, and Effect of Money

Written by
KEVIN MILLER

Illustrated by
GARY LOCKE

A Faith Building Guide
can be found on page 32.

Equipping Kids for Life
faithkids.com

Faith Kidz is an imprint of Cook Communications Ministries,
Colorado Springs, Colorado 80918
Cook Communications, Paris, Ontario
Kingsway Communications, Eastbourne, England

First printing, 2003
Printed in Singapore.
1 2 3 4 5 6 7 8 9 10 Printing/Year 07 06 05 04 03

Library of Congress Cataloging-in-Publication Data
Burkett, Larry.
        All about money / Larry Burkett ; illustrated by Gary Locke.
                p. cm.
1. Money—Religious aspects—Christianity—Juvenile literature.
2. Finance, Personal—Religious aspects—Christianity—Juvenile literature.
3. Money—Juvenile literature. 4. Finance, Personal—Juvenile
literature. [1. Money—Religious aspects—Christianity. 2. Finance,
Personal—Religious aspects—Christianity.] I. Locke, Gary, ill. II. Title.
        BR115.W4 .W86 2002
        241'.68—dc21

                                2001006708

Stewardship for the Family
Executive Producer: Allen Burkett

Lightwave Publishing
Concept Direction: Rick Osborne

Cook Communications Ministries
Senior Editor: Heather Gemmen
Designer: Keith Sherrer, iDesignEtc.
Design Manager: Jeffrey P. Barnes

CONTENTS

WHAT IS MONEY?

This sounds like a simple **question,** doesn't it? Money is the change in your pocket, the bills in your wallet, the balance in your bank account, right? Well, to some people it is. But to other people, money can come in the form of giant stones, tiny seashells—even cocoa beans! That's because money isn't a particular object; it's more like an idea. For this reason, it's actually easier to explain what money *does* than what money *is*. Anything can serve as money as long as it does the following three things:

Money should make it easier to exchange things. Before money was invented, people used the *barter* system. With this system, if you had a pig but needed some flour, you found some-

one who had flour but no pig—and traded with him. But if no one wanted a pig, you had to go without flour. (Plus, you were stuck carting around your pig until you found someone who wanted it.) But once the concept of money was invented, you could sell your pig to the butcher and then take that money to the local miller to buy a sack of flour. The miller could then take that money to the butcher and buy some bacon. The butcher could take it to the tailor and buy a suit, and so on.

Money should help you compare the value of things that are quite different. Which is worth more: a pound of bacon or a pound of flour? How would you decide? Money makes this task simple. We can say the bacon is worth $2 and the flour is worth 50¢. How is this determined? By how much it costs to manufacture each product, how much of each product is available for sale, and how big the demand is for each product.

Flour can go bad and pigs can get sick!

Finally, money should help you keep track of how much wealth you have. You can keep track of your wealth in all sorts of ways, including real estate, stocks, bonds—even animals. But money is one of the best ways to store and keep track of wealth, because, unlike these other *assets* (things you own), it costs nothing to store and you can use it immediately. With the other assets, you have to sell them before you can use that wealth to buy other things. Plus, flour can go bad and pigs can get sick. With money, you don't have these problems.

HOW IS MONEY MADE?

Ever heard the saying, "It's worth a mint!"? That's what people say about something that is extremely valuable. They say this because a *mint* is where coins are manufactured. Can you imagine how rich you would be if you owned a money factory?

We've got some bad news for you: You can't. Only governments are allowed to manufacture money. People who make their own money are called *counterfeiters*. Only the government is allowed to make money because if there is too much money in circulation, it soon loses its value. It's a simple rule of supply and demand: the more common something is, such as sand, the less valuable it is. But the more scarce something is, such as gold, the more valuable it becomes. Therefore, the government has to walk a fine line between preserving money's availability and its value.

COINS

Coins are made by heating metal strips and pressing them into thin sheets. American pennies are made from copper-coated zinc; nickels from a mixture of copper and nickel; and dimes, quarters, half-dollars, and dollars from three layers of copper and nickel pressed together. These sheets are then cut into blank coins, just like you cut cookies out of dough. Then the coins are heated and cleaned before the designs are stamped on them. Stamping a coin takes over 40 tons of pressure!

BILLS

In the United States, bills are made by the Bureau of Engraving and Printing using special paper and complicated designs to make them difficult to copy. The paper is a secret mixture of cotton and linen. The inks are top secret as well.

The paper is run through printing presses in huge sheets, much like newspapers are printed. The images for each bill are engraved into steel printing plates that are kept under very high security. These printing plates are coated with ink and then stamped onto the bills in the printing press. Once the bills are printed, they are cut and bundled into packages ready to be sent off to the banks.

FACTOID

Funny Money

Do you know how to tell the difference between a real $20 bill and a fake one? Counterfeiters are betting you can't. They try to make their own money by carefully trying to copy the designs, inks, and papers used by the government. Many bills have been redesigned in recent years to make counterfeiting even more difficult.

Counterfeiting is a serious offense. If you're caught making your own money, you can get up to 15 years in prison and a $5,000 fine—and that has to be paid in *real* money.

"The safest way to double your money is to fold it over once and put it in your pocket."

EARLY FORMS OF MONEY

People haven't always used bills and coins as money. As we mentioned earlier, before money was invented, people used the barter system, trading pigs for lumber, lumber for food, food for clothing, and so on. But this system only worked on a small scale, providing you could find someone who had what you wanted and wanted what you had. Eventually someone got the idea of giving someone a token or a note instead of the actual thing they wanted. This way, if you wanted to trade your pig for flour but the miller had all the bacon he could use, you could just give him a token, like an "IOU," that said he could come by and get the pig when he needed it. The token didn't have any value. It only stood for something that had value: the pig.

Soon, people realized that if everyone agreed to use the same token, they could simply trade tokens to get the things they wanted. For example, if the miller gave you enough flour to equal one pig, you gave him ten tokens, which also equalled one pig. The miller could either bring these tokens back to you and

exchange them for the pig or, if he wasn't in the mood for pork chops, take them down to the market and buy some fruits and vegetables. This token is what we now call money.

Giant stone wheels for money?

FACTOID

Strange Types of Money Throughout History

Throughout history, people have used all sorts of tokens for money. The Yap Islanders in the South Pacific used giant stone wheels with holes cut in the middle. Some of these stood 12 feet tall and weighed 500 pounds! Other people have used sharks' teeth, feathers, and even braids of hair.

Sometimes the tokens used for money had value in and of themselves, such as gold or cattle. At other times, people used common objects, such as shells or beans, to keep track of their wealth. But rare and valuable items worked best because they weren't easy to get or copy. For instance, if a society used cocoa beans for money, there was nothing stopping people from simply picking more beans and increasing their wealth.

Governments eventually took control of the money system so this couldn't happen. Now the only money that is valid is money the government supplies.

HOW WE GOT OUR MONEY SYSTEM

Today, we use a mixture of coins and paper bills as money. Ever wondered why?

COINS

Before coins were invented, people used pieces of gold and silver as money. Because every piece was a different size and shape, they each had to be weighed to determine their value.

But weighing chunks of metal was a tedious job. So eventually the king of ancient Lydia came up with a better idea. He started making pieces of gold mixed with silver (called *electrum*) and stamped them to show their weight and purity so everyone knew what they were worth. Now no one had to weigh the metal; they just had to look at the stamp.

Later, these bits of metal were flattened and transformed into coins. Alexander the Great, conqueror of the Persian Empire, was the first ruler to put his face on a coin. This started a trend that has continued into the present day all around the world.

BILLS

Paper money was first invented by the Chinese about 1,000 years ago. Europeans and Americans didn't start using it for another 700 years.

In the beginning, this money was just simple pieces of paper with the amount written on them. People could then trade in these notes for "real" money: gold or silver coins. But as paper money became more accepted, it was decorated with elaborate drawings and designs much like our paper bills today. Now every bill is a work of art.

INFLATION

Bills were originally "backed" by gold and silver. For every one-dollar note the government issued, it had one dollar's worth of gold in the bank. This was called the "gold standard." The paper merely represented the value of the gold. But eventually governments left the gold standard behind and started issuing money based on how much they thought was needed. So people began to view paper money as having value in and of itself. Money now "floated;" that is, it was no longer tied to an "anchor," like gold, that could determine its value.

If our money is just cheap pieces of paper and metal, what gives it value? The simple answer is: the government says it is valuable and everyone else agrees.

When people disagree about the value of money, that is, when they think there is an oversupply of money in the system, you get something called *inflation*. This means that today, one dollar won't buy you what it did 30 years ago; people raise their prices to compensate for the falling value of money. Don't believe it? Just ask your parents how much a candy bar cost when they were kids and compare it to the price of one today.

(To see how the value of money has changed over time, go to the inflation calculator at the Federal Reserve Bank of Minneapolis's web site: **woodrow.mpls.frb.fed.us**)

Inflation happens when the supply of money is greater than the demand, making it less valuable, or when something, such as war, threatens a country's economy.

Inflation is unavoidable due to constant changes in our economy and money supply. We measure inflation by averaging how much the price of goods and services increases over time. This is called the *inflation rate*. The government tries to keep this rate within reasonable levels, usually between 2–3% per year. That means in 30 years, the candy bar you buy for 50¢ today could cost $15! Instead of earning an average income of $35,000, you will probably be earning more like $105,000.

CAN YOU SPARE SOME CHANGE?

Have you ever taken a close look at the coins in your pocket? A really close look? Okay, then whose face is on the front of an American quarter? No peeking! If you said George Washington, you're right.

Take a closer look at your pocket change on these pages and find out what all those pictures and words really mean.*

PENNY

(from the British word "pence")

Front

• "In God We Trust" was first used on the two-cent coin in 1864. Since 1955, the phrase has appeared on all U.S. coins and bills.

• Abraham Lincoln, 16th President of the United States (1861-1865)

• "Liberty" is one of the greatest values of the United States.

• A letter located below the date indicates which mint the coin came from. Below are the four mints and their marks:

Mint	Mark
Philadelphia	P (or no mint mark)
Denver	D
San Francisco	S
West Point	W

Back

• "E pluribus unum" is a Latin phrase meaning, "One out of many." It comes from the Great Seal of the United States designed by Benjamin Franklin, John Adams, and Thomas Jefferson on July 4, 1776. The motto represented the union of the 13 original states.

• Lincoln Memorial, located in Washington, D.C.

• "One Cent" indicates the value of the coin.

NICKEL

(named after one of the metals it is made of)

Front

• 5 cents

• Thomas Jefferson, third President of the United States (1801–1809)

Back

• Monticello "Little Mountain," Jefferson's home in Albemare County, Virginia

DIME

(from the Latin
word "decimus," which means "one tenth")

Front

- 10 cents
- Franklin D. Roosevelt,
  32nd President of the
  United States (1933–1945)

Back

- Liberty torch with sprigs of olive (representing peace) and oak (representing victory)

QUARTER

(so named because it is one
quarter of a dollar)

Front

- 25 cents
- George Washington,
  first President of the United
  States (1789–1797)

Back

- The bald eagle is the official bird of the United States. As of 1999, this design is being replaced by 50 new designs that represent the 50 United States.

HALF-DOLLAR

Front

- 50 cents

- John F. Kennedy, 35th
  President of the United
  States (1961–1963)

Back

- Presidential Coat of Arms

DOLLAR

Front

- 100 cents
- Sacagawea, the young
  Shoshone interpreter
  who assisted Lewis and
  Clark in their expedition
  from the Great Northern Plains
  to the Pacific Ocean and back (1804–1806)

Back

- Bald Eagle, official
  bird of the United
  States

BILLS, BILLS, & MORE BILLS

You probably never thought there was so much to learn about pocket change. Well, that's nothing compared to bills. Redesigned in 1996 to make them more difficult to counterfeit, American bills are much more than fancy printed papers—they're high tech equipment!

BILL FEATURES

This note is legal tender for all debts, public and private: This phrase must appear on every U.S. bill. It gives people confidence that they can use the bill to pay their debts or measure what is owed to them.

In God We Trust: This phrase first appeared on the two-cent coin in 1864. Since 1955, this phrase has appeared on all U.S. bills and coins.

Signatures: All currency is signed by the Secretary of the Treasury and the Treasurer of the United States. Over time, the people who hold these positions change, so not every bill has the same signature on it.

Series: This date marks the first year a new bill design was used. This date is not necessarily the same as the year the bill was printed. Smaller design changes are marked by a letter after the date (for example, 1996A).

Serial number: Bills are like snowflakes: no two are alike. They can all be identified by their serial number.

E pluribus unum: This Latin phrase, which means "One out of many," appears on all U.S. bills and coins.

Portrait: A portrait of a different historical president or leader appears on every bill.

Fine-line printing patterns: These appear on both sides of the bills in the background of the portrait and the buildings. This type of printing is difficult for counterfeiters to copy.

Some extra features on newer bills follow:

Watermark: A copy of the portrait appears off to one side when held up to the light.

Security thread: An embedded plastic strip is placed in a different spot for each denomination. You can see the strip by holding the bill up to a bright light. Use a magnifying glass to see the letters USA, the denomination of the bill, and, on the $50 and $20, a flag.

When placed under ultraviolet light, the strip glows a different color for each denomination.

Color-shifting ink: The number in the lower right hand corner on the face of the bill appears green or turns black, depending on the angle you look at it.

Microprinting: Microprinting is tiny print that can be read only with a magnifier, and it becomes blurred when copied. It appears in a unique place on each denomination.

Low-vision feature: The number on the back of the bill has been made larger and a machine-readable feature has been added for the blind so they can identify the bill using a scanning device.

Federal Reserve Bank Seal: The 12 Federal Reserve Banks distribute all U.S. bills for circulation. Before 1996, a seal from an individual Federal Reserve Bank was printed on each bill. Beginning with the $100 bill in 1996, a general seal that represents the entire Federal Reserve System replaced individual bank seals. The letter on the seal matches the district number of that bank. The district number is also located in the four corners of the bill. The letter on the bill, located just below the serial number also tells you which bank distributed the note.

FACTOID

We have many nicknames for money. Here are the origins of a few of them:

Cash: a word the ancient Chinese adopted from the Portuguese caixa (pronounced "cash-a") to describe a bundle of 100 coins

Bucks: a throwback to the time when Indian tribes used deerskins for trading

Moolah: comes from the jazz community in the 1920s and 1930s

Bread or Dough: comes from the saying, "If you don't work, you don't eat."

Two bits: comes from old Spanish coins called "pieces of eight"—brittle coins that could be broken up into eight pieces. Two "bits" equalled one quarter of the whole, just like our 25-cent coin today.

HOW BANKS WORK

It may seem natural for your parents to deposit money in the bank and then take it out again when they need it. But have you ever wondered why your parents do this?

A bank is basically a safe place to store money. A bank can be anything from a ceramic pig to a sock drawer to a building on the corner—any place where your money won't get damaged or lost.

But the building on the corner, the bank we're talking about, does more than simply store money. It also lends money. And, unlike your piggy bank, it pays you to keep your money there. In other words, banks allow you to make money with money. Now how good is that?

The money banks pay you is called *interest*. Interest is a fee paid to you for the privilege of "renting" your money while it's in the bank. When people put money in the bank, they usually don't need it all right away. So someone else who needs money can "rent" some of that extra money in the form of a loan. When banks loan money, they charge interest. The bank keeps some of this interest for itself as profit and gives the rest back to the people whose money they lent out—people like you!

Interest is calculated as a percentage of the total amount of money or *balance* you owe or have in the bank. For example, if you have $1,000 in your account at 12% interest, you will earn $120 in interest by the end of the year ($1,000 x .12 = $120).

Banks allow you to make money with money.

FACTOID

The "Miracle" of Compound Interest

There are two main types of interest: *simple interest* as described above, which is calculated yearly, and *compound interest* which is calculated daily, weekly, monthly, or quarterly (every three months). Of the two types, compound interest is the best, because it allows you to earn interest on your interest.

Take the $1,000 at 12% example from above. If this interest was compounded monthly, you would receive one percent per month. That means after one month, you would earn $10 interest. This amount would be added to your original $1,000. The interest on the second month would then be calculated on $1,010, not just $1,000. At the end of the year, you will have earned $137.97—$17.97 more than you would have earned through simple interest!

CREDIT CARDS, LOANS, & DEBT

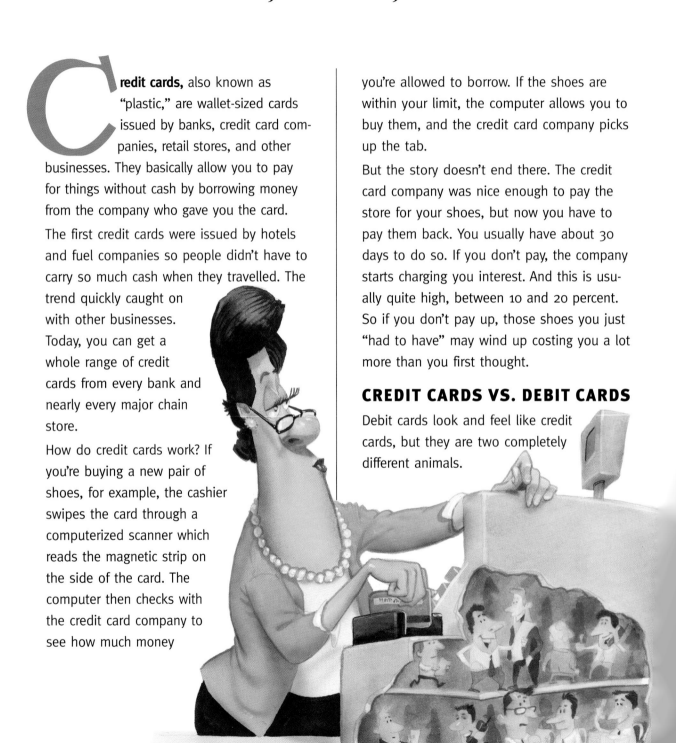

Credit cards, also known as "plastic," are wallet-sized cards issued by banks, credit card companies, retail stores, and other businesses. They basically allow you to pay for things without cash by borrowing money from the company who gave you the card.

The first credit cards were issued by hotels and fuel companies so people didn't have to carry so much cash when they travelled. The trend quickly caught on with other businesses. Today, you can get a whole range of credit cards from every bank and nearly every major chain store.

How do credit cards work? If you're buying a new pair of shoes, for example, the cashier swipes the card through a computerized scanner which reads the magnetic strip on the side of the card. The computer then checks with the credit card company to see how much money

you're allowed to borrow. If the shoes are within your limit, the computer allows you to buy them, and the credit card company picks up the tab.

But the story doesn't end there. The credit card company was nice enough to pay the store for your shoes, but now you have to pay them back. You usually have about 30 days to do so. If you don't pay, the company starts charging you interest. And this is usually quite high, between 10 and 20 percent. So if you don't pay up, those shoes you just "had to have" may wind up costing you a lot more than you first thought.

CREDIT CARDS VS. DEBIT CARDS

Debit cards look and feel like credit cards, but they are two completely different animals.

The main difference between them is that debit cards only allow you to spend money you already have, while credit cards allow you to spend money you don't. You also don't have to pay back the money you withdraw with a debit card, and you don't have to pay interest on it either. That's because you're not borrowing it. All you're doing is giving the bank's computers permission to withdraw money from your account and pay the store.

Visa,® a major credit card company, has come out with a new card especially for teenagers, called VisaBuxx.® It combines the features of a credit and debit card by allowing you to put money on the card and then spend it until all of it is gone. This way you have the convenience of a credit card without the danger of going into debt!

FACTOID

Don't Be a Slave to Debt!

Proverbs 22:7 says, "The rich rule over the poor, and the borrower is servant to the lender." You don't want to forget this verse when it comes to credit cards and loans. Remember: the more money you borrow, the less freedom you have, because you have to keep slaving away to pay off your debts. Many people today fall into the trap of borrowing more than they are able to pay back. But it's better to save towards the things you want and then buy them. That way, while you are saving money, the bank is paying you interest rather than you paying them.

But the story doesn't end there.

DIFFERENT COUNTRIES, DIFFERENT CURRENCIES

The American dollar may be the most widely accepted *currency* (form of money) in the world, but it isn't the only one. Every country or region has its own form of money. Here are a few samples from other English-speaking countries.

CANADA

Just like America, the basic unit of Canadian currency is the dollar. However, the Canadian dollar no longer comes in the form of a bill. As of 1987, it was replaced by a bronze-colored coin, nicknamed "the loonie" after the loon which appears on the face of the coin. Canadians also have a two-dollar coin nicknamed "the twonie," introduced in 1996. Higher Canadian denominations come in the form of bills—including five, ten, twenty, fifty, one hundred, and one thousand- dollar denominations. They also have fifty-cent pieces, quarters, dimes, nickels, and pennies.

AUSTRALIA

Australian money shares many of the same aspects as its American

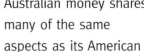

and Canadian cousins. For one thing, their basic unit of currency is also the dollar. And, like Canada, Australia has replaced its one and two-dollar bills with coins (in 1984 and 1988 respectively).

The other bank notes and coins used by Australians are similar to those used in Canada and the United States except for one thing: In 1992, the Australian government started removing one and two-cent coins from circulation. Now the smallest Australian coin in circulation is the five-cent piece.

It just goes to show that a penny really won't buy what it used to, especially in Australia!

GREAT BRITAIN

The basic unit of British currency is the pound sterling. It gets its name from the fact that it used to represent one pound of silver. Up until 1971, one pound could be broken down into 20 shillings of 12 pence (or pennies) each. A penny could be further broken down into four farthings. Today, one pound simply equals 100 pence. The pound sterling comes in the form of a coin. Britain also has a two-pound coin. The rest of its coins are similar to those in America, Australia, and Canada, except that they use "pence" instead of "cents." Therefore, they have a one-pence coin, a two-pence coin, and so on.

The American dollar isn't the only one.

THE FUTURE OF MONEY

As you've seen, money has gone through some tremendous changes throughout history. But that's nothing compared to where it's going from here.

Big changes are already happening. Today, we still use bills and coins to buy things. But technology is making this less and less necessary. Now you can earn, save, invest, and spend money without ever actually seeing or handling it. For example, your parents can have their employer direct-deposit their paycheck in the bank. They can also have this money automatically withdrawn to pay bills or to go to charity. All they ever see of it is the numbers on their bank statement. It's fast, clean, and painless.

The Internet is also changing the way we think about money. Now we can pay bills, transfer funds, and send and receive cash at nearly the speed of light to anyone in the world—and we never have to handle a coin or a bill or seal an envelope. Some companies are also issuing "cyber money," electronic money that can only be used on the Internet.

Some people question whether or not moving to a completely electronic form of money is wise or safe. On the plus side, electronic money is easy to store—it's just numbers in a computer's memory! It's also quick and convenient. No one has to worry about having actual cash on them anymore. You just pull out the plastic and, *voila*!

On the negative side, computer crime and credit card fraud are becoming more common as people break through the banks' security systems and steal enormous amounts of money. These people are difficult to catch because few people have this level of computer ability.

Whatever the case, it seems that money is continuing to move quickly towards becoming completely electronic. One day, all we may have is a card, a computer chip, or simply a number that accesses all of our financial information.

It's fast, clean, and painless.

HOW TO MAKE MONEY

Don't worry; this isn't a chapter on counterfeiting! By "making money" we mean *earning* money, not printing $100 bills in your basement. You can earn money in one of three ways:

GET A JOB

The most common way people earn money is by getting a job. With a job, you make an agreement with an employer to trade some of your time for some of her money. How much money you get for your time depends on the difficulty of the job and the qualifications, skills, and experience you bring to the table. The more difficult the job and the more experience, skills, and education you

have, the better you are paid. If you don't think you're making enough money at your job, there are two ways to change this: work more hours or increase the value of your time by getting more education or learning new skills.

START A BUSINESS

Another popular way of earning money is to start your own business. People who do this are called *entrepreneurs*. A business can be anything—from window washing to a clothing store to a computer repair service. You can own a big business where you

skill and years of learning and experience to do it successfully. You also need to earn and save the money before you invest it.

employ a lot of people, or you can simply work out of your home. The key to having a successful business is offering a product or service for which people are willing to spend their money.

INVEST YOUR MONEY

Many people earn all or part of their income by investing money in stocks, bonds (a loan given to a company or the government), or real estate. By investing, you don't actually produce or do anything. You let your money do the work for you by lending it to someone else who makes it grow. This is a great way to make money, but it takes tremendous

FACTOID

Start Your Own Business

Why not start your own business right now? This is a great way to start learning how money and business works. What skills can you use to make money? Can you rake leaves? Mow grass? Shovel snow? Wash windows? Baby-sit? Ask your parents to help you get started, possibly by making up flyers or putting an ad in the local paper.

OTHER THINGS YOU CAN DO WITH MONEY

Okay, you've got a job, started a business, or invested some money and made a profit. Congratulations! But now that you have money, what can you do with it?

SPEND IT

The first thing most people want to do with money is spend it. You might want to buy new clothes, a video game, or maybe some tasty snacks. You can spend your money on basically two main things: wants and needs. Wants are things you would like to own but can do without. These include things like toys or candy bars. Needs are things you can't do without. These include things like paying *bills* (money

you owe) and buying shoes, school supplies, and so forth. You should always make sure all of your needs are met before you spend money on your wants.

SAVE IT

It's fun to spend money, but it's always wise to keep some back for emergencies or for a time when you aren't earning money. You can also save money so that you are able to afford more expensive items that you want or need—such as a bike, a new pair of designer jeans, or education after high school. University or college may seem like a long way off, but it will come sooner than you think!

BIG OL' BURGER
COLORADO SPRINGS
12347

PAY TO THE ORDER OF CINDY LEW $150.00
ONE HUNDRED AND FIFTY AND 00/100

GIVE IT

Giving money to people who don't have enough to meet their needs or to charitable organizations that rely on donations to survive is also a good thing to do and something that God requires of us. A good rule of thumb is to give the first part of your money, usually 10%, to your church. This is called a *tithe*, which means "one tenth." You can give away more than 10% of your money if you like, but this is a good place to start.

FACTOID

Be a Wise Spender

Everyone has a limited amount of money to spend. So you should try to make the most of the money you have. This means that before you spend money, you should shop around, compare prices, and make sure you're getting the best value for your dollar. Remember: the cheapest item is not always the best! Things are usually cheap for a reason: they're poor quality. But often items that cost more are really no better. Do yourself a favor and research the product you want to buy. The goal is to come up with the best *value* for your money: the best quality at the best price.

MANAGING YOUR PENNIES, NICKELS, DIMES, & QUARTERS

Have you ever heard the saying "Look after your pennies, and the dollars will take care of themselves"? This saying means that if you manage small amounts of money wisely, over time they will turn into larger amounts.

This saying is based on a biblical principal called *stewardship*. Stewardship is another word for management. Stewards or managers don't really own anything. They merely take care of things that belong to others. Because God created everything, everything belongs to him. That means everything you have belongs to God as well, even though you may have worked hard to earn the money to buy it. So that makes you a steward—God's steward.

In the Bible, God promises that if we are faithful in the little things, such as how we handle our pocket change, he will put us in charge of larger things, such as houses and vehicles (Matthew 25:14–30). God starts us out with small amounts of money so we can practice how to handle it. Once we learn some basic money management skills, he trusts us with more.

When God asks us to spend our money wisely, he isn't trying to take away our fun. He does this because he knows that if we don't spend our money wisely, we're going to wind up in a heap of trouble. He also knows that if we give to others, it will help make everyone's life better. God wants us to have a good life, full of all sorts of wonderful things (John 10:10). The way to have that life is to learn God's wisdom and apply it.

He isn't trying to take away our fun.

FACTOID

What Are You a Steward Of?

Even though you're still young, God has already put you in charge of many things. Look around your bedroom. You probably have clothes, books, toys, and many other items. You can start practicing your stewardship skills right now by taking good care of these things. For example, if you've outgrown some clothes, why not wash and fold them and give them to someone else who can use them? You can also put your toys away when you're done playing so you don't accidentally step on them and break them. How else can you be a good manager of the things you're in charge of?

MANAGING YOUR BIG & LITTLE BILLS

So you know you should manage your money wisely. But how can you do this? The best way is to come up with a plan for your money. This plan is called a *budget*. A budget helps you keep track of every dollar and cent you earn, save, spend, invest, and give. Best of all, budgeting will help you make sure you never spend more than you earn.

You can start budgeting right now even if you only earn a few dollars per month. The Budget Tracker (facing page) can help you do this. If you look at it, you will see that it divides your money up into four categories: Giving or Tithing, Short-term Savings, Long-term Savings, and Spending.

As we recommended earlier, it is a good idea to put the first 10% you earn into your Giving or Tithing category. This should go to your church. The next 25% goes into Short-term Savings. This money can be used for things that will take a month or two to save up for, such as a T-shirt or a book. The next category, also 25%, is for Long-term Savings. This is for larger items, such as a new soccer ball or a paint set. Finally, we have Spending. Forty percent of your money should go into this category. You can use this money for whatever you want. But remember: needs first, wants second.

MONEY: YOUR BEST FRIEND OR YOUR WORST ENEMY

You should pretty much be an expert on money by now. You know what money is, how it's made, how to make it yourself, and what to do with it when you get it. Money is good in that it allows you to get the things you need and to help others who don't have enough. But the Bible also says, "The love of money is a root of all kinds of evil" (1 Timothy 6:10). People do all sorts of terrible things because they think money is more important than people, relationships, and God. Money is a great tool, but if you allow it to become too important, you're in for disappointment—you'll never have enough to satisfy you. Instead, you should trust God to look after all of your needs and make loving him, not earning money, your most important goal.

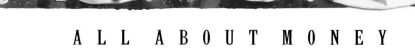

BUDGET TRACKER

| Date | GIVING/TITHING (10%) | | SHORT-TERM SAVINGS (25%) | | LONG-TERM SAVINGS (25%) | | SPENDING (40%) | | Total All |
	Transaction	Balance	Goal: Transaction	Cost: Balance	Goal: Transaction	Cost: Balance	Transaction	Balance	Balances

Faith
Building
Guide

Ages
9 and up

Stewardship

ALL ABOUT MONEY

Spiritual Building Block: Stewardship

You can become better managers of your money in the following ways:

Think About It:

What do you tend to do when you have money: do you hoard it away, do you get things for your-self right away, do you buy all your friends a milkshake; do you invest some, do you share some, do you spend some, do you save some? Think honestly and carefully about your skills as a money manager, noting both your strengths and your weaknesses. Pray that God will help you to make the right choices and have the right attitude about money.

Talk About It:

Chat with some of your friends about money. Ask for their advice on how to improve your money-managing skills in the areas that are hard for you; offer advice in those areas you do well. Encourage each other day by day: If someone has a hard time saving money, don't talk him into going shopping with you; if you hate to share, ask your friends to help you find a ministry that does some really great stuff so you can be excited about sharing. The Bible says that God will give you wisdom if you ask for it.

Try It:

Decide ahead of time how you want to use your money. Make a plan. Ask your parents to help you develop a budget that is appropriate and realistic. And then stick to it. (In other words, if you are tempted to take a little money from long-term savings to meet a short-term need, resist.) As you develop into a good money manager, you will gain a healthy self-confidence and a life-long skill. More than that, you will be assured that you are pleasing God by being a good steward of the many things he gives you.